MYSTERIES
OF THE ANCIENT WORLD

THE KNIGHTS TEMPLAR

NICHOLAS BEST

WEIDENFELD & NICOLSON

LONDON

On a March day in 1314, after seven years of torture and imprisonment, two old men were dragged in chains through the streets of Paris. Followed by a jeering crowd, they

*This Crusader
mural can be
seen at the Templar
chapel in Cressec.*

were hustled towards one of the islands in the Seine.

There they were stripped to their underwear before

being tied to a stake set up close to the great cathedral

of Nôtre Dame.

3

The Templars' Curse

The men were Geoffrey de Charney and Jacques de Molay. They were respectively the Preceptor of Normandy and the Grand Master of the Order of the Knights Templar. They were about to burn to death for a host of alleged crimes – including sacrilege, blasphemy, sodomy, Devil worship and the practice of Black Magic.

But there was still time to repent. Even as the firewood was heaped around them, the two men were given every chance to confess their sins. If they confessed, they would not have to die. They would be taken back to prison instead, back to a slower, more lingering punishment in solitary confinement, left to rot in the dark with their legs in irons and no prospect of ever being released. Other Templars had chosen solitary confinement instead of death. De Charney and de Molay could too, if they wished.

Both men refused. They would not admit to worshipping the Devil. They protested their innocence instead, renouncing confessions they had made earlier under torture, insisting that they had always been innocent in the eyes of God. They were prepared to die now, if that was His will, rather than admit to the charges against them.

A final attempt was made to dissuade them. Red hot coals were shovelled around them, slowly roasting them alive. There was still a chance to change their minds, still an opportunity to save themselves from the fire.

King Philip watches as Geoffrey de Charney and Jacques de Molay are burned at the stake.

The men were adamant. The Grand Master asked that his hands should not be tied, so that he could die in prayer. He asked that his body should be turned on the stake, that he might see Notre Dame one last time before the end. His wishes were granted and the fire was lit. The two men observed it without flinching. They were calm and composed, perfectly prepared to meet their Maker.

Gradually the fire took hold. As the flames rose, the Grand Master raised his eyes to Heaven and uttered a curse. It was a loud curse, resonant, full of anguish; a curse heard not only by the spectators on the island but by all of France, a curse that echoed down the centuries and was remembered by Frenchmen everywhere, even as late as the French Revolution. It was a curse on the enemies of the Templars – on the Pope who had condemned the Order, on King Philip of France who had persecuted its members, on everyone who had ever opposed the Knights Templar, whoever they might be: 'Let evil overcome those who have condemned us!' the Grand Master swore. 'God will avenge our death. God will grant justice. Let our enemies suffer, as we have suffered, for what they have done!'

The crowd shrank from the Grand Master's words. Even as they did though,

The cathedral of Nôtre Dame in Paris, scene of the execution of de Charney and de Molay.

the flames were gathering pace. The Grand Master's voice cracked and died, was heard no more. His body began to bubble and blacken, his flesh melting from his bones as it disintegrated in the fierce heat. The Preceptor's flesh melted too. Before long, nothing was left of either of them except a few charred bones and a heap of ash still too hot to touch. The two men were dead. With them, for all practical purposes, had died the 200-year-old Order of Knights Templar.

That night, after the fire had cooled and the crowd had dispersed, a group of sympathizers stole across to the island and quietly retrieved the bones of the two martyrs for proper burial elsewhere.

Thirty-three days later the Pope died. A few months after that, King Philip too lay dead and France was plunged into anarchy and chaos for the next 100 years. The curse of the Grand Master had been amply fulfilled.

Who were the Templars?

What kind of people were these Templars? Were they the simple warrior monks they professed to be? Or were they the Devil worshippers of legend, the mysterious idolaters and sorcerers who roasted their own children, performed secret midnight rituals with animals and were guilty of every kind of sexual malpractice? Which of these versions is true?

Their origins were simple enough. They were fighting men, Frankish knights who had fought in the First Crusade and accompanied the victorious army to Jerusalem. There they had banded together in 1118 to form an order of warrior monks, pledged to protect the lives of pilgrims travelling to the holy places.

After capturing Jerusalem in 1099, the crusaders killed thousands of Moslems before looting the city.

The Dome of the Rock overlooks Jerusalem's Temple of Solomon, from which the Knights Templar took their name.

There were only nine Templars to begin with, led by Hugh de Payens and Geoffrey of St Omer. They were all devout, all committed to poverty, chastity and obedience. From the first, though, they differed from other religious orders in that they were specifically military in character, a body of fighting men wholly dedicated to the defence of the Christian faith. They differed also from military organizations in their poverty and humility, always wearing shabby clothes instead of the traditional finery expected of warrior knights.

*C*rusader Godfrey de Bouillon was elected King of Jerusalem in 1099, but refused the title as an act of piety.

*T*he French religious leader St Bernard inspired the early Templars to a life of austerity and sanctity.

At first, there was nowhere to house this unique Order, but accommodation was soon found beside the Dome of the Rock and the western wall, two of Jerusalem's most sacred places. The accommodation was built on the supposed site of the Temple of Solomon. It was from this that the Knights Templar got their name.

They prospered at once, for there were no regular troops in the Holy Land. The crusader armies had gone home after Jerusalem was captured, leaving

re la terre sainte z le puy
re ypistiens y demourãs
ussent secourus et gardes
ntre ses impetueux assaulx
e seurs tresanciens et anciez
nemis. et ouurant se tresoz
fassi se donna plain pardon
remission de puine z de
ulpe de tous pchies atoute
a vng chasain de ceulx qi

en faueur et pour audier la ter
re sainte prendroient lenseigne
de la sainte Croix z yroient
en cellui voyage. Et combien
que yeust loze es diuerses
parties de ypistiente plusieur
seigneurs ducs z prelats
Toutesffois selonc pour
lesui temps lestoient comme
lestoient iournal au point du

*K*rak de
Chevaliers
*at Homs, in
Syria, a crusader
stronghold.*

only a motley garrison to defend the holy places against Moslem attack. The Knights Templar offered to fill this gap. Their offer was accepted with alacrity.

They needed money to help them, because defence of the Holy Land did not come cheap. There were castles to be built, strong-points, barracks for the troops. Accordingly, money was raised from every country in Christendom – so much in fact that although Templars personally were never well off, their Order eventually became enormously rich, far richer than it needed to be for its original intended purpose.

Nevertheless, the Templars provided value for money – at first, anyway. They fought hard throughout all the subsequent crusades and could always be counted on when they were needed. That their efforts met with only mixed success was hardly their fault, for the Christians in the Holy Land found

Many Templars joined the crusade to Damietta, in upper Egypt, the gateway to the granary of the Nile.

*A*fter Saladin
*captured
Jerusalem in 1187,
the Templars never
set foot there again.*

themselves against increasingly stiff opposition as time wore on – not least from the Moslem forces led by Saladin, ruler of Egypt. After many years of struggle, he finally captured Jerusalem in 1187. The Templars were ousted from their original home and forced to decamp. They remained in the Holy Land until 1303, but they were never again to set foot in Jerusalem, the city they had sworn to defend with their lives.

By then however, the Order had changed considerably in character. What had begun as a simple body of fighting men was now far more complex and sinister. After many years of handling the finances needed for the crusades (the cash was kept safe in Templar castles), they had become bankers and money-men as well as soldiers – the most sophisticated bankers in all of Europe. They had become property owners, owning 9,000 manors in many different lands. They had become religious dignitaries, enjoying special immunities granted to them by the Pope. Yet they remained still a law unto themselves, a mysterious society swearing allegiance always to each other, rather than to any king or country: a society with no apparent reason for existence after its expulsion from the Holy Land.

Saladin, King of Egypt, was the crusaders' most formidable opponent, but a very chivalrous foe.

As the chief bankers of Europe, the Templars frequently used seals on important documents.

Templar in his home outfit.

Templar in his war outfit.

The Persecution of the Templars

This was obviously a recipe for disaster. A rich and secret society, powerful, arrogant, forbidden to women, yet meeting only behind closed doors and accountable to no one but itself. It was inevitable that jealousies should arise about the Templars, that rumours should begin to spread. And spread they eventually did, all across Europe.

How far the rumours were true, and how far they were merely a trumped-up excuse to seize the Templars' vast wealth, is impossible to say at this distance. What is certain though is that the rumours were lurid in the extreme, varying from heresy and witchcraft to kissing the anus of a black cat and sleeping with the Devil in the guise of a beautiful woman. There was talk of mysterious initiation ceremonies in which men kissed each other on the lips, the navel and the buttocks. It was said also that Templars would spit on the Cross and worship the Devil in a darkened room; that the ashes of their dead were given to new Templars

Templar effigies in a London church. The Temple underground stop is named after their Order.

Romanticized 19th-century portrait of a Templar.

25

This 13th-century Templar castle is at Ponferrada in Spain.

to eat; that virgins were made pregnant and their new-born babies roasted over a fire, the fat being used to anoint the Templars' satanic idols. In a superstitious age, these were very serious accusations indeed.

Perhaps the most serious accusation of all was that the Templars had deliberately abandoned the Holy Land to the Moslems, surrendering to their enemies in a pact with the Devil designed to preserve the Templars' own power and wealth. It was certainly true that they had formed alliances with Moslems in the interests of peace and religious tolerance. They were also suspected of worshipping the devil Baphomet in various forms (usually a jewelled skull, a wooden phallus or an androgynous winged idol, part-woman, part-goat).

The devil Baphomet, perhaps a corruption of Mahommed, was considered by many to be the Bible's Beast of Revelation.

An engraving of a Templar in travelling dress from a 1585 woodcut.

*T*emplar manors, such as this at Les Andelys in
France, provided a constant source of income.

Baphomet was held to be a corruption of the name Mohammed, and Mohammed was considered by Christians to be the Beast of Revelation, distinguished by his mark and the number 666.

But what really undid the Templars was their money. They had become seriously rich by the beginning of the 14th century: so rich in England, for example, that Templars there were able to make a substantial contribution towards Edward I's wars against France. This naturally did not go down well with the French, in particular King Philip of France. He was an ambitious monarch, devious and scheming, but desperately short of finance of his own and, in a

*U*nder pressure from King Philip, Pope Clement dissolved the Order of Templars at Vienne in 1312. turbulent reign, had already debased the coinage several times and expelled the Jews from France, confiscating all their property. By 1307, he was again in urgent need of cash. He looked around for a fresh source of finance – and his eye fell on the Templars.

Their spies had warned them that trouble was coming, but the extent of it came as a shock. They were arrested on the morning of Friday 13 October – all 5,000, every Templar in France. The arrests were co-ordinated so that only a handful escaped, perhaps 20 in all. The rest were rounded up and thrown into prison, even the Grand Master and his officials. The Templars were supposed to enjoy immunity from arrest, but their immunity did not help them now. The Pope owed his position to King Philip and did nothing to save them. Neither did anyone else. Even by the standards of the day, it was an infamous act of betrayal.

The ordinary people of France were deeply disturbed by it. These were holy men, not common criminals. Whatever they had done – and not everyone believed they were in league with the Devil – the Templars should not have been treated thus. It was not the way things were supposed to happen.

Philip's fellow monarchs were not impressed either. He wrote to all his neighbouring kings, explaining his action and inviting them to do the same to their own Templars. Few followed his lead; they did not share his view of the Templars' guilt. It was not until the Pope issued a Bull commanding them to abolish the Order that they complied, and then only with considerable reservations.

Philip however remained adamant. Under French law, the Templars were guilty until proved innocent – and the charges

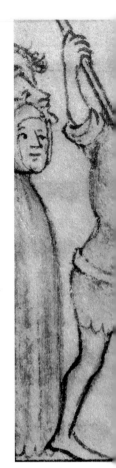

against them were vile in the extreme. Sodomy, obscenity, sacrilege: the king saw to it that the allegations received widespread publicity after the Templars' arrest, the full enormity of their excesses exposed for the first time. He obtained confessions too, from the Grand Master among others, confessions under oath to the vilest depravities imaginable. The Grand Master personally admitted to spitting on the Cross, and other diabolical offences. He begged forgiveness, publicly urging his fellow Templars to follow suit while they still had the chance.

The Grand Master had been tortured, of course, as had the others. In Paris

*A*fter refusing to confess, 54 *Templars were burned in a single afternoon, outside Paris.* alone, 36 Templars died of the effects within a few days of their arrest. Some were starved and beaten, their feet burned until only the bones remained. Others were stretched on the rack until their arms and legs popped out of their sockets, or subjected to the strappado – dropped on a rope with their arms tied behind their back, until their shoulders broke under the strain. Few ultimately refused to confess.

Some Templars did refuse however, a brave and resolute minority. Fifty-four of them were burned at the stake one afternoon, in a field outside Paris.

Others disappeared into dungeons, never to be seen again. It was seven years before the last of them had been tried and disposed of. The process was supposed to come to a climax with the public confession of the Grand Master and the Preceptor of Normandy at Nôtre Dame. In the event though, both men used the occasion to retract their confessions, reaffirming their innocence in front of a crowd of thousands. They were put to death at once, and the Order of the Knights Templar was heard no more.

The Legacy of the Templars

But the Templars were not forgotten. Their properties were confiscated, their Order expunged and those who were not killed or imprisoned scattered far and wide. Yet the idea they represented was too powerful to be extinguished

*A*rdchattan Priory in Scotland was one of many Templar properties in the British Isles.

*T*emplar chapels were built all over Christendom. This one is at Mücheln, near Wettin, in Germany.

altogether. Their Order was resurrected in the 18th century and given a new lease of life as part of the clandestine brotherhood of Freemasonry. Knights Templar have continued as Freemasons ever since.

They were almost certainly innocent of the charges levelled against them by King Philip, but it was the sheer enormity of the offences that has lingered in the public mind, rather than the Templars' denials. Guilty or not, the Templars are always remembered for what was alleged about them, rather than for anything they actually did.

Dante, their contemporary, was in no doubt as to where the guilt should lie for the Templars' demise. In his *Divine Comedy*, he took the Pope and King Philip and put them firmly where they belonged for what they had done – in Hell.

The Templars had revenge, of a sort. In 1793, almost five centuries after the Grand Master's curse, Louis XVI was sent to the guillotine in Paris. His death effectively marked the end of the French monarchy, a long line of despots of whom King Philip had been only one. After Louis had been executed, it is said that a man came forward from the crowd and dabbled his hands in the blood. The man was a Freemason. He was taking revenge for what had happened to his Templar forebears so many centuries before. Justice, at long last, had been done.

*T**he execution of Louis XVI was seen by contemporary Freemasons as the fulfilment of the Grand Master's curse of 1314.***

KNIGHTS
TEMPLAR

PHOTOGRAPHIC ACKNOWLEDGEMENTS
Cover AKG London; pages 2–3 Ancient Art &
Architecture [AAA]; p. 4–5 Fortean Picture
Library [FPL]; pp. 6–7, 8–9 e.t. archive [ETA];
pp. 14–15 Zefa; pp. 16–17 AAA;
pp. 18–19, 20 ETA; p. 21 FPL;
pp. 22, 23 FPL/Dr. Elmar G. Gruber;
p. 24 Michael Jenner; p. 25 AKG; pp. 26–7 AAA;
pp. 28, 29 FPL; pp. 30–31 AAA; pp. 32–3 FPL;
pp. 34–5 AKG; p. 36 FPL/Andreas Trottmann;
pp. 37, 38–9 AKG.

First published in Great Britain 1997
by George Weidenfeld and Nicolson Ltd
The Orion Publishing Group
5 Upper St Martin's Lane
London WC2H 9EA

A CIP catalogue record for this book is available
from the British Library
ISBN 0 297 823124

Picture Research: Suzanne Williams

Design: Harry Green

Typeset in Baskerville